BELUGA WHALES

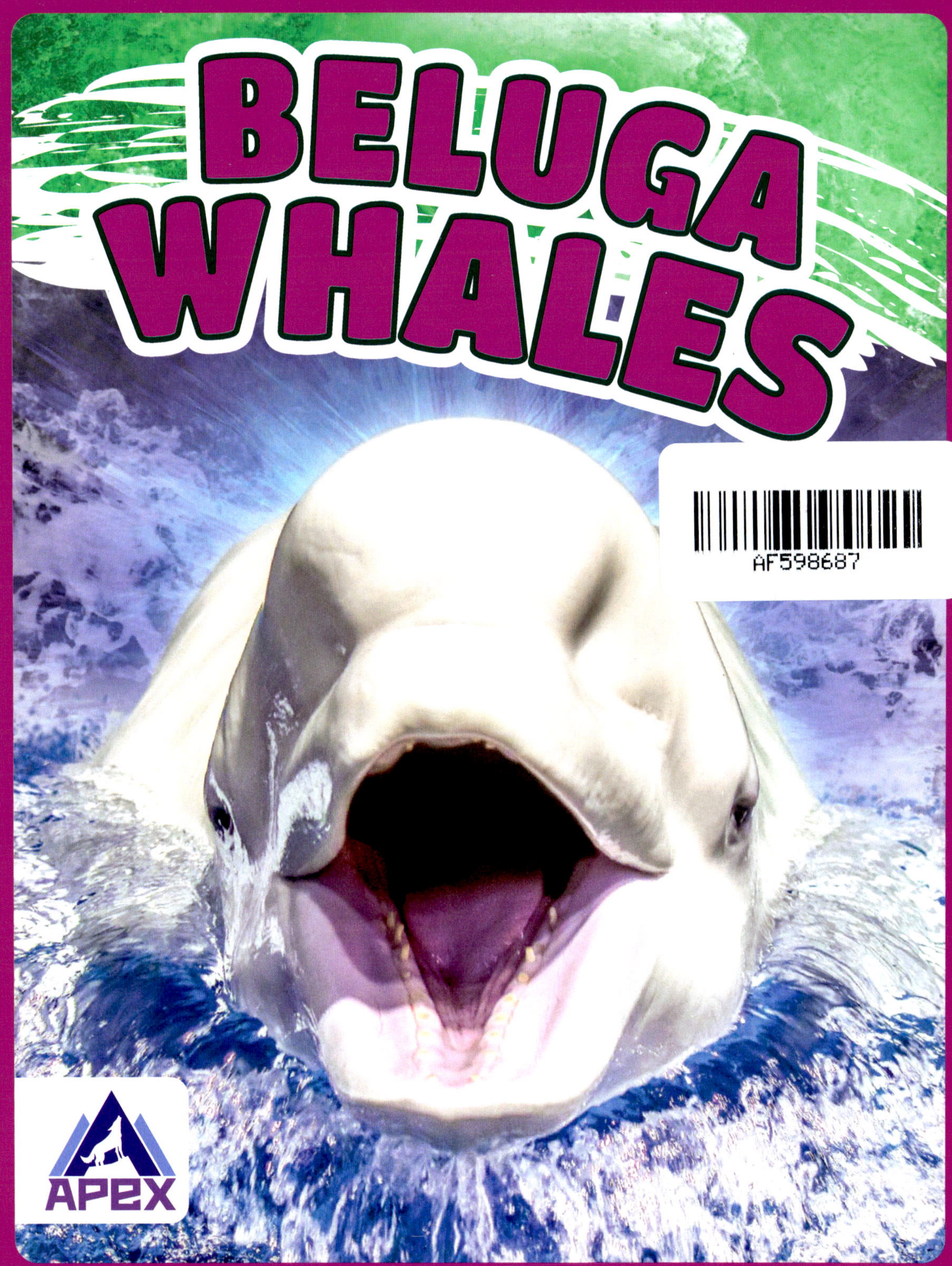

BY ANGELA LIM

WWW.APEXEDITIONS.COM

Apex is distributed by North Star Editions:
sales@northstareditions.com | 888-417-0195

Produced for Apex by Red Line Editorial.

Photographs ©: Shutterstock Images, cover, 1, 4–5, 10–11, 12, 14–15, 16–17, 18–19, 20–21, 26–27, 29; iStockphoto, 6–7, 8–9, 12–13, 22–23, 24, 25

Library of Congress Control Number: 2020952973

ISBN
978-1-63738-001-7 (hardcover)
978-1-63738-037-6 (paperback)
978-1-63738-108-3 (ebook pdf)
978-1-63738-073-4 (hosted ebook)

Printed in the United States of America
Mankato, MN
082021

NOTE TO PARENTS AND EDUCATORS

Apex books are designed to build literacy skills in striving readers. Exciting, high-interest content attracts and holds readers' attention. The text is carefully leveled to allow students to achieve success quickly. Additional features, such as bolded glossary words for difficult terms, help build comprehension.

TABLE OF CONTENTS

CHAPTER 1

ICY WATERS

The beluga whale swims in the Arctic Ocean. It flaps its strong tail. It goes deep underwater.

A beluga whale dives into the cold waters.

Arctic waters can get as cold as 28 degrees Fahrenheit (–2°C).

The dark water is very cold. But the whale has thick skin. It stays warm.

A beluga whale's skin is 100 times thicker than human skin.

Beluga whales often start growing teeth after they are one year old.

The whale is hunting for fish. It makes clicking noises. The sounds bounce off fish. Then the sounds **echo** back to the whale. They tell it where the fish are. Then the whale can catch and eat them.

ECHOLOCATION

Using sound to find objects is called **echolocation.** Belugas use this sense to find food. They can hunt in the dark. They can also find holes in the ice.

CHAPTER 2

LIFE IN THE ARCTIC

Beluga whales have **adapted** to life in the Arctic. Their white color blends in with their icy **habitat**. And their thick skin keeps them warm.

A beluga whale swims near an iceberg.

Belugas are **mammals**. They can't breathe underwater. They must come to the surface for air. They breathe through a hole on the top of their head.

A beluga whale comes to the surface for air.

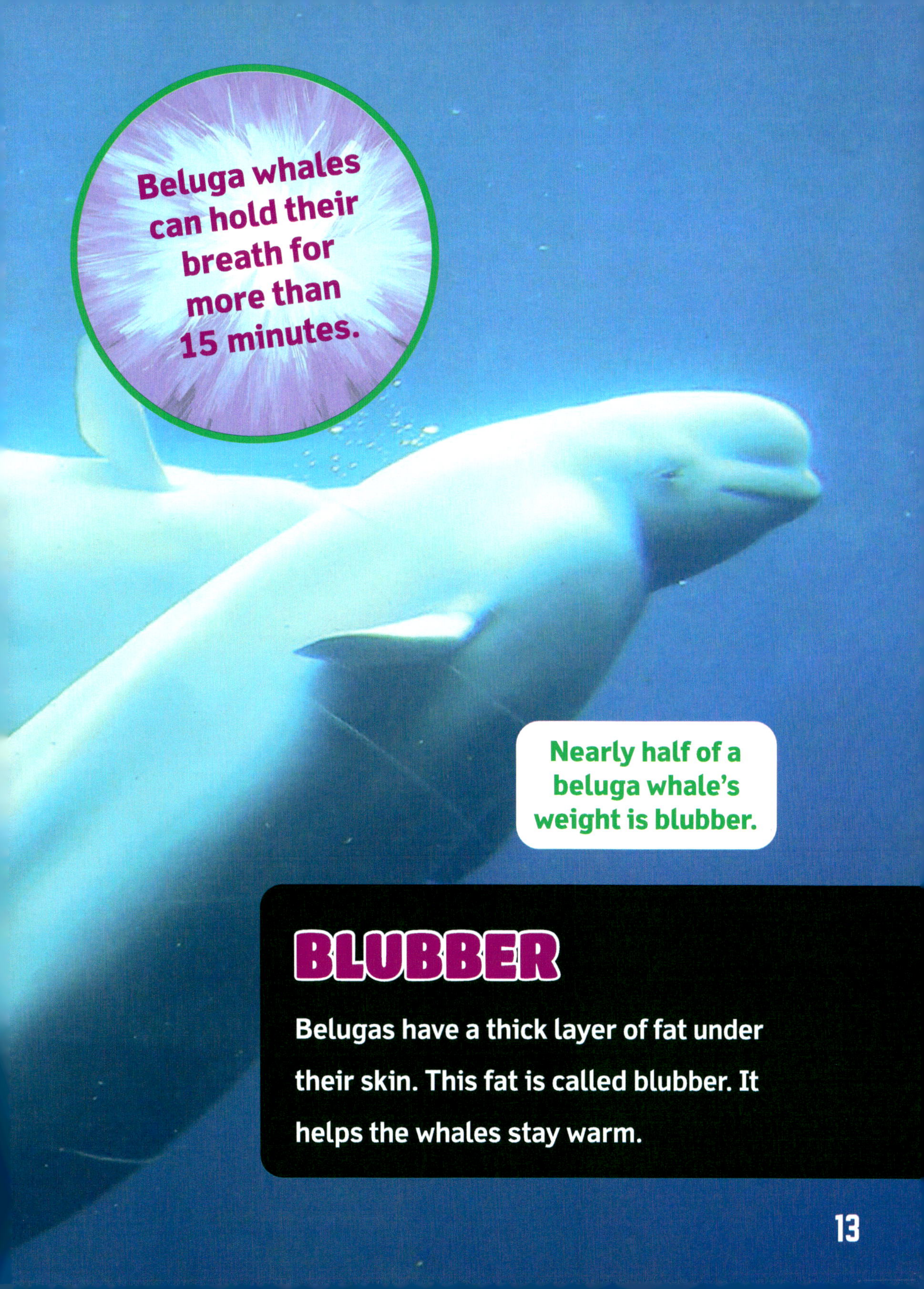

Beluga whales can hold their breath for more than 15 minutes.

Nearly half of a beluga whale's weight is blubber.

BLUBBER

Belugas have a thick layer of fat under their skin. This fat is called blubber. It helps the whales stay warm.

A young beluga stays close to its mother.

Belugas also have live babies. A baby whale is called a calf.

Newborn beluga whales are dark gray. This color fades as they grow up.

CHAPTER 3

SOCIAL ANIMALS

Beluga whales live in groups called pods. The whales swim and hunt together. Most pods have just a few whales. But pods often grow as whales **migrate**.

Beluga whales live together in groups.

Belugas migrate two times each year. In the fall, ice forms in the Arctic. Belugas swim to warmer waters. They come back in the spring when the ice melts.

A single migrating pod can have hundreds of beluga whales.

Curious beluga whales swim close to a diver.

A beluga sprays a stream of water.

Belugas **communicate** using many sounds. The whales chirp, squeak, and whistle. These sounds carry through the water.

MELON

A melon is a mound of fat on a beluga's head. The whale can change the melon's shape. Different shapes help the whale make different sounds.

Belugas are playful. Sometimes they blow bubbles underwater.

CHAPTER 4

FINDING FOOD

Beluga whales eat more than 100 types of animals. These animals include fish, shrimp, and octopuses. Sometimes belugas suck up food from the ocean floor. Other times, they hunt close to the surface.

Belugas sometimes have to dive deep underwater to find food.

Groups of belugas chase **prey** such as fish. Then they trap the prey in **shallow** waters.

Flatfish are one type of fish that beluga whales hunt.

Belugas often make quick dives for food before returning to the surface.

TOOTHED WHALES

A beluga whale's mouth has 30 to 40 teeth. The teeth look like small pegs. The whale does not use its teeth to chew. Instead, it uses them to grip prey.

Beluga whales don't chew their food. Instead, the whales swallow their food whole.

Beluga whales can swim backward and make tight turns around sea ice.

The shape of a beluga's mouth makes it look like it's smiling.

COMPREHENSION QUESTIONS

Write your answers on a separate piece of paper.

1. Write a sentence that describes the main ideas of Chapter 2.

2. Would you want to live in the Arctic? Why or why not?

3. What helps keep a beluga whale warm?

   A. its melon
   B. its blubber
   C. its pod

4. Why do beluga whales need to find holes in the ice?

   A. They look for food beneath the holes.
   B. The water is warmer near the holes.
   C. They need to be able to come to the surface and breathe.

5. What does **carry** mean in this book?

*The whales chirp, squeak, and whistle. These sounds **carry** through the water.*

A. to travel
B. to hold
C. to support

6. What does **grip** mean in this book?

*The whale does not use its teeth to chew. Instead, it uses them to **grip** prey.*

A. to hold tightly
B. to chew loudly
C. to run away

Answer key on page 32.

GLOSSARY

adapted

Changed to fit a new situation.

communicate

To send and receive messages.

echo

To bounce off a surface as a sound.

echolocation

The ability to use sound to locate objects.

habitat

The type of place where animals normally live.

mammals

Animals that have hair and produce milk for their young.

migrate

To move from one part of the world to another.

prey

Animals that are hunted and eaten by other animals.

shallow

Not deep.

TO LEARN MORE

BOOKS

Furgang, Kathy. *Beluga Whales*. New York: Enslow Publishing, 2020.

Polinsky, Paige V. *Humpback Whale: Marvelous Musician*. Minneapolis: Abdo Publishing, 2017.

Rathburn, Betsy. *Beluga Whales*. Minneapolis: Bellwether Media, 2021.

ONLINE RESOURCES

Visit **www.apexeditions.com** to find links and resources related to this title.

ABOUT THE AUTHOR

Angela Lim lives in Minnesota. She thinks sea creatures are fascinating.

INDEX

Answer Key:
1. Answers will vary; **2.** Answers will vary; **3.** B; **4.** C; **5.** A; **6.** A